Journal

Belongs to:

_____

_____

_____

Published by Better World Press, Inc.
A Division of Your True Nature, Inc.
P.O. Box 272309, Fort Collins, Colorado 80527
800-992-4769 email: branch@yourtruenature.com
yourtruenature.com

Original silk painting cover and tree Illustrations: Ilan Shamir
Woodcut river illustrations: Chuck Black
Library of Congress Cataloging-in-Publication Data
ISBN: 9 781930 175396
    Shamir, Ilan, 1951-
            Advice from a River / Ilan Shamir
            1. Rivers
            2. Human Growth and Potential
            3. Nature
            4. Health and Wellness

Printed in the USA on recycled paper. Many thanks to the trees for
their gift of paper! All paper used in the printing of this book has been
replanted through the 100% Replanted program.
Visit www.ReplantTrees.org.

Suggestions for using the
Advice from a River Journal

Rivers invite us to reconnect with the stream of life, the wisdom of nature, and our own well-being. The river itself guides us to *Go with the flow . . . Slow down and meander . . . and Delight in life's adventures around every bend!*

Remember to take time to get close to the earth and its many moving waters—mighty rivers, sparkling mountain streams, and winding creeks. As you sit near a river, let your imagination drift and allow its wisdom to trickle in and comfort you. Let the natural flow of water pick you up and carry you into a stream of creativity. Take the time to write and sketch and bring to life your thoughts and musings. The best way to start journaling is to just start. Like the river, your words and ideas will pick up a natural momentum. *Just go with the flow of your own true nature.*

You can use this river journal any way that works for you. Here's one idea of how to let the words guide you . . . Nineteen of the journal pages have a line from the "Advice from a River" poem. On the "Go with the flow" page, and the blank pages that follow, you could make note of ideas for how to go with the flow in your life instead of trying to "push the river" to create what you want. The "Slow down and meander" pages invite you to take in a breath of fresh air and relax. For the "Stay current" pages, record your thoughts about ways to let go of the things you no longer need or want and let them flow downstream and out of your life.

Regardless of how you use this journal, always remember . . . Rivers are inspiring friends and teachers of wisdom. Find a river and let its graceful waters guide you . . . *because the beauty is in the journey!*

Inspired by the river . . .

I stand beside the river, watching the light
playfully dance over the moving water.
I am reminded so simply and gracefully of my
own true nature . . . moving, flowing,
serene, and on course.

Sure, there are those days when it feels like I am fighting
the current, swimming upstream, and longing for the
simplicity of life. Yet, I know this isn't the natural flow.
Sometimes, life is just turbulent and rocky.
The river, with its symphony of sounds, plays its music.
I listen with my full being to its timeless message
and breathe in its soothing voice.
My tightness loosens. I feel connected and delighted
as I let the river wash my cares away.
I delight in knowing I can return to the river
again and again
to feel its serenity,
to hear its music,
and to be in the presence of its clear wisdom.

Ilan Shamir

Advice from a River

Dear Friend . . .
Go with the flow!
Be thoughtful of those downstream
Slow down and meander
Be clear
Follow the path of least resistance
for rapid success

Immerse yourself in nature:
trickling streams,
roaring waterfalls,
sparkles of light dancing on water

Delight in life's adventures
around every bend

Let difficulties stream away

Live simply and gracefully in
Your own true nature . . .
moving, flowing,
allowing,
serene and on course

Rough waters become smooth
If you find yourself babbling . . . just smile!
It takes time to carve the
beauty of the canyon
Go around the obstacles
Stay current

The beauty is in the journey!

Dear Friend . . .
Go with the flow

Be thoughtful
of those downstream

Slow down and meander

Be clear

Follow the path of
least resistance
for rapid success

_____

_____

_____

_____

_____

_____

_____

_____

_____

_____

Immerse yourself in nature:

_____

_____

_____

_____

_____

_____

_____

_____

_____

_____

trickling streams,

roaring waterfalls,

sparkles of light
dancing on water

Delight in life's adventures
around every bend

Let difficulties stream away

Live simply and gracefully in
your own true nature . . .

_____

_____

_____

_____

_____

_____

_____

_____

_____

moving, flowing, allowing,
serene and on course

Rough waters become smooth

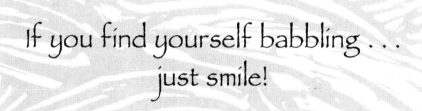

If you find yourself babbling . . .
just smile!

It takes time to carve
the beauty of the canyon

Go around the obstacles

Stay current

The beauty is in the journey!

_____

_____

_____

_____

_____

Ilan Shamir's
Advice Book Series

 Advice from a Tree &
Accompanying Journal

 Advice from a River &
Accompanying Journal

 Advice from a Mountain &
Accompanying Journal

 Advice from a Garden

 Advice from Nature
(Includes Advice from a Sea Turtle,
Owl, Canyon and many more)

More Advice from Nature
(Includes Advice from a Moose,
Wildflower, Night Sky and many more)

Other Titles

Tree Celebrations-
Planting and Celebrating Trees

PoetTree-
The Wilderness I Am

Simple Wisdom-
A Thousand Things Went Right Today!

The True Nature of Designing and
Promoting Successful Products

The True Nature of Designing and
Promoting Successful Programs

My Colorado
Nuggets of Wit and Wisdom

Words

*We invite you to visit us at:
yourtruenature.com for hundreds of other
items including collectable frameable art
cards, bookmarks, posters, mugs, magnets,
t-shirts and more.*

Keynote programs
Breakouts
Workshops

Through the simplicity and beauty of trees and nature, Ilan Shamir calls us to branch out, grow, and celebrate our true nature! Author of the bestselling Advice from a Tree products and "A Thousand Things Went Right Today," Ilan's inspiring programs are a perfect addition to conferences and events.

Member of the:
*National Associaton for Interpretation
*National Speakers Association Colorado
*National Storytellers Network

yourtruenature.com

Have a Tree Planted for Someone Special!

Your purchase price of $8.95 for one tree, or $18.95 for a three-tree grove, plants and cares for native trees in projects in El Salvador, Honduras, Costa Rica, and Nicaragua through the nonprofit organization Trees, Water & People. The recipient gets a beautiful personalized greeting card from you, and both you and the recipient can visit the planting area online!

A simple gift that lasts a lifetime!
It's as easy as 1, 2, TREE . . .

Qty ($8.95)	Qty ($18.95)	Occasion
___	___	All Occasion

(Friendship, birthday, Mother's Day, thank you, birth, anniversary, congratulations, Father's Day, wedding, graduation)

___	Holiday
___	Memorial

Your Name _____
Address _____
City/State/ZIP _____
Email _____
Telephone _____

Total Qty _____ at $ 8.95 = $_____
Total Qty _____ at $18.95 = $_____
Shipping $ 6.50
GRAND TOTAL $_____

Send with your check to:
Your True Nature, Inc. Box 272309
Fort Collins, CO 80527, (970)282-1620
Email: orders@yourtruenature.com
Visit our website for more information or to order online at yourtruenature.com